The moral law

Its place in Scripture and its relevance today

John L. Mackay

CHRISTIAN INSTITUTE

CHRISTIAN INFLUENCE IN A SECULAR WORLD

This publication is based on two lectures delivered by the author for The Christian Institute's Autumn Lecture series in November 2003 at St Stephen's Church, Elswick, Newcastle upon Tyne.

Copyright © The Christian Institute 2004

The author has asserted his right under Section 77 of the Copyright, Designs & Patents Act 1988 to be identified as the author of this work.

First printed in October 2004

ISBN 1 901086 27 5

Published by The Christian Institute
Wilberforce House, 4 Park Road, Gosforth Business Park,
Newcastle upon Tyne, NE12 8DG

The Christian Institute is a Company Limited by Guarantee, registered in England as a charity. Company No. 263 4440, Charity No. 100 4774.
A charity registered in Scotland. Charity No. SC039220.

Contents

Foreword

Many Christians are very confused today about the relationship between the Old and New Testaments. In the 1960s it became fashionable to believe that Christ replaced Law with love. Some say that we can dispense with the moral law because "we are not under law but under grace". In this publication Professor John L. Mackay of the Free Church of Scotland College, shows how this view cannot be squared with the teaching of the Bible.

John Mackay shows that the Bible teaches that the moral law still applies and is bound up with God's glory, His nature, His salvation purposes and with the preservation of ordered life following the Fall.

Throughout Church history there have been those who opposed this view – those who say that the moral law is no longer binding on Christians. They are antinomian – which means literally in Greek 'against' (anti) 'law' (nomos). This teaching is not new. The Apostle Paul tackled it in his letter to the Romans. The Puritans also tackled antinomianism in their day, indeed it was they who first labelled this false teaching as 'antinomianism'.

Today a quiet and subtle brand of antinomianism, in all but name, has tiptoed into too many of our evangelical churches arm-in-arm with a twisted view of love, grace and liberty. Such confusion and compromise in the church is bound to have a disastrous effect on the world as the salt looses its saltiness. Professor Mackay rightly points out that perhaps never before has there been such a basic rejection of the Ten Commandments.

It is vitally important that Christians think through the relationship between the Old and the New Testaments. Many are under the impression that Old Testament believers were saved by works through keeping the law. John Mackay shows how wrong this view is – they, like us, are saved by grace through faith. Having been justified by faith we, like believers in the Old Testament Church, need the moral law to show us how to live.

As Samuel Bolton put it "the law sends us to the Gospel, that we may be justified, and the Gospel sends us to the law againe to enquire what is our dutie being justified."[1]

Theologians down the ages, and especially the Reformers, have made the very helpful distinction that the Bible contains three types of law: the moral, the civil and the ceremonial. The *ceremonial* laws have been fulfilled in Christ. The sacrifices no longer need to be made as Christ has offered himself on the cross in our place. The *civil* laws of Israel are not necessarily binding on people and nations today. But the *moral* law has not been done away with. It is still in force and binding on everyone whether a believer or unbeliever.

This 'threefold division' of the law was taught by Aquinas but clearly it has roots that go back even further. Augustine taught that the law was not uniform and the moral and symbolical parts of the law must be clearly distinguished.[2] The threefold division was also one of the touchstones of the Reformation about which all the Reformers agreed. Article VII of the Thirty Nine Articles of the Church of England (1571) states:

> "Although the Law given from God by Moses, as touching Ceremonies and Rites, do not bind Christian men, nor the Civil precepts thereof ought

> of necessity to be received in any commonwealth; yet notwithstanding,
> no Christian man whatsoever is free from the obedience to the
> Commandments which are called Moral"

In other words, the ceremonial laws have been fulfilled in Christ and are no longer binding, the civil laws of Old Testament Israel are not necessarily applicable in the nation state (or commonwealth), but the moral law still applies.

Similarly, chapter 19 of the Westminster Confession of Faith (1643-46) teaches that:

> "The moral law doth for ever bind all"; the "ceremonial laws are now
> abrogated under the New Testament"; and the "sundry judicial" (or civil)
> laws of Israel "expired together with the state of that people, not obliging
> any other now, further than the general equity thereof may require".[3]

Not only did the Reformers teach about the three *types* of law, but they also taught that there were three *purposes* of the law: to restrain sin (the civil or political use), to teach that man is guilty before God and in need of a saviour (the pedagogic use) and to show Christians how to live (the normative use).

As the Lutheran Formula of Concord (1576) states:

> "It is established that the Law of God was given to men for three causes:
> first, that a certain external discipline might be preserved, and wild
> and intractable men might be restrained, as it were by certain barriers;
> secondly, that by the Law men might be brought to an acknowledgement
> of their sins; thirdly, that regenerate men, to all of whom, nevertheless,
> much of the flesh still cleaves, for that very reason may have some certain
> rule after which they ought to shape their life". Article VI

In 1944 T C Hammond, the author of *In Understanding Be Men*, pointed out that "*The Reformation Leaders* (1500-1600) brought to the Church as great an ethical as doctrinal deliverance. This fact has not always been fully appreciated by Christian people."[4] How we need such an ethical and doctrinal deliverance today!

We need to regain a biblical view of the moral law. There is an urgent need for evangelicals to understand what the Bible says about it. There needs to be teaching – teaching that is clear, logical, powerful and biblical. Christians need to know not just *what* the law says, but *why* the law says it. In the Autumn of 2003 Professor Mackay delivered two outstanding lectures for The Christian Institute. Both lectures examined the Ten Commandments, showing their place in Scripture and their relevance today. This publication is based on those lectures.

I urge you to read Professor Mackay's booklet. Then read it again. Then teach it to others.

Colin Hart
Director
The Christian Institute
August 2004

Endnotes

[1] Bolton, S, *The True Bounds of Christian Freedome* (1645) quoted in Kevan, E *The Grace of Law*, Soli Deo Gloria, 1997 (2nd ed), pages 175-176

[2] Bayes, J, *Reformation Today*, September – October 2000, 177, pages 3 - 10

[3] The Westminister Confession of Faith, Chapter 19, paras III, IV and V

[4] Hammond, T C, *Perfect Freedom*, IVF, undated edition (originally published in 1938), page 35

Introduction

It is arguably the case that the Ten Commandments are more neglected in Britain today than they have been for centuries. Given that is so, it is not unreasonable to probe why this has come about. Obviously a root cause for the absence of the Ten Commandments from our national life is general abandonment of Christianity. This aversion to Biblical religion is compounded by prevailing contempt for authority in any form. Since the beginning of the Enlightenment in the eighteenth century respect for norms and standards has been steadily undermined. The scepticism of Enlightenment thinkers first became evident in their argument that it is not possible for mankind to use divine law as an external standard for judging human laws and conduct. Initially there was an attempt to substitute some other basis for discerning what constitutes a universal natural law. Their aim was to establish an objective criterion for determining what is right and what is wrong. However, that too has been abandoned. The prevailing consensus is that there is no external norm which sets out the principles to which human laws and conduct ought to conform. All that matters is what the majority or the most powerful group in a society wants. The fundamental criterion has been taken to be man, and all standards are relativised. The strident notes of the rebel are heard at every level of society: "We are free to do our own thing, and who are you to tell us otherwise?" Fyodor Dostoyevsky put it this way: "If there is no God, everything is permitted."

What is more lamentable is that the same focus on mankind as determining moral norms has increasingly pervaded Christian thinking. Indeed, it may be argued that in large measure it was within the Church that abandonment of the absolute standards of God's Word (the Bible) in fact arose. Although the Church itself often seemed astonishingly unaware of it, others were quick to spot the hypocrisy of a body urging moral standards upon society as a whole when it had itself so largely come to disbelieve the Bible from which those standards are derived. The Church has no more moral authority than any other group in society if it fails to ground its beliefs, practices and standards in the Word of God. We are living in an age when the Christian Church is largely ineffective because its attitude to the norms of God's Word has brought it under the judgment of God. It is as if he is saying to us, "You thought you could undermine and set aside my Word and still be effective as my church witnessing in this world. Well, I will let you experience what happens when you spurn my way. I will let you see just how persuasive and compelling you can be on the basis of your own ideas."

The fundamental predicament is the age-long problem of authority. Mankind is in rebellion against God, and rebels repudiate God's authority over them. The spirit of rebellion and antinomianism (lawlessness) has infiltrated the Church. It was not a difficult task as the moral flaw in our nature is such that each of us naturally wants to go our own way and determine appropriate parameters for our own conduct. Our inherent predisposition towards such an attitude has been compounded by the lack of certainty within the Church about the place and role of God's law. Are not the Ten Commandments Old Testament teaching, a relic from a former age, and no longer of relevance? Are they not negative and gloomy, and should not New Testament religion be joyful and positive? Does not the New Testament clearly say, "We are not under law but under grace"? Surely Christian conduct is to be determined by the norms of love, not by innumerable petty restrictions?

My aim in this booklet is to address such questions and to show the role that the moral standards of God's Word should have not only in the life of the Christian church, individually and collectively, but also in the development of national policy and in providing norms for personal conduct throughout society.

The Old Testament evidence

I make no apology for beginning by turning to the Old Testament for our basic orientation on the role of law. We do, of course, go to the Old Testament as Christians. It is our privilege to read its promises and the development of them in the light of their fulfilment in Jesus Christ. However, to come to a full appreciation of what is in the New Testament we must follow the example of the early church and view the epochal transformation brought about by the life and ministry of Jesus Christ against the background of the Old Testament promises which he fulfilled. The same procedure is equally relevant to our consideration of law. We must begin at the beginning.

In looking back at the place of law in the Old Testament, it is natural to focus on the Ten Commandments. These are to be found in Exodus 20. The setting is Mount Sinai. There God instituted his covenant with the Israelites whom, under the guidance of Moses, he had brought out of the oppression and slavery of Egypt. The Ten Commandments were then revealed as God's standards for the on-going life of his people.

But that on its own is not enough to locate the Ten Commandments theologically. We need to set the Mosaic covenant instituted at Sinai in terms of the whole sweep of divine dealings with humanity. Since the Fall of mankind, alienation and estrangement have characterised the relationship between God and man. No longer is there the close and continuous fellowship which had been enjoyed in Eden. Mankind was expelled from the Garden, and though God was not silent, he no longer talked freely or continuously with those he had created in his image and likeness. Certainly the human race was not utterly abandoned; God revealed himself to a chosen few here and there over the ages. But things are not as they once were. Even though there has been material advance, the course of human history is characterised by spiritual corruption and violence.

The early period of God's dealings with mankind climaxed in the call of Abraham. Unnoticed by the world at large, something new was inaugurated. The way forward in God's dealings with humanity would no longer be with the human race as a whole. Revelation would be associated with a special people — Abraham and his descendants. By divine determination the way of salvation was graciously made known to them. The promise was given that God would be their God and provide for them — "And I will establish my covenant ... to be God to you and to your offspring after you" (Genesis 17:7).[1] And God would also provide through them — "In you all the families of the earth shall be blessed" (Genesis 12:3). Abraham the man of faith accepted God at his word — "And he believed the LORD, and he counted it to him as righteousness" (Genesis 15:6). He put his trust in the promise of divine provision.

Now it is significant that the focus of Abraham's faith was particularly in the divine promise regarding 'offspring' or 'seed' (Genesis 15:5). That is not simply a matter of the existence of progeny for Abraham, nor indeed of how numerous they would be. Ever since mention was made in Genesis 3:15 of 'the seed of the woman' through whom God would bring deliverance to fallen humanity, 'seed'/ 'offspring' had been virtually a technical term relating to divinely promised salvation from sin and evil. The content of the promise grew and was clarified over time. But it was in God's promised deliverance that the faith of the Old Testament church rested. That is why Abraham's attitude of trust was accepted by God as putting Abraham in a right relationship with him. He took God at his word and looked forward to the promised deliverance. That is why he is the father of the faithful in every age (Romans 4:16). His relationship with God was not on the basis of what Abraham had personally accomplished ('works'), but on the basis of trust in the revealed promise of God ('faith').

Furthermore, we may note that, though the focus of revelation and salvation had been narrowed to one man and one family line, the universal scope of divine blessing was not thereby negated. It was narrowed down so that it might in due time effectively spread out. "Through your offspring all nations on the earth will be blessed" (Genesis 22:18).

But then in God's providence the family of covenant blessing is brought down to Egypt and for four hundred years there is divine silence. It is not, however, the case that the promise is in abeyance. The family increases in size; they become a nation. But they are a nation oppressed and enslaved until the time came in God's plan for his purpose to move forwards once more.

Again we must note that, as in the case of Abraham, the basis of divine action is grace, not reward. Remember the historical situation. By the time of Moses many powerful empires had emerged in the ancient world. In Egypt, in Mesopotamia and among the Hittites there were nations that had military might, commercial enterprises, art and literature, splendid architecture—and pagan darkness. The nations had lost sight of the one true God. They were dazzled by their own achievements. They were in thraldom to the powers of spiritual darkness.

And was the situation any different among the people with the covenant promise, held in servitude in Egypt? Alas, no! They too had largely forgotten the God of their fathers and were worshipping idols. The bondage imposed on Israel in Egypt was the penalty for their own sin. There is repeated Scriptural testimony that in Egypt the Israelites became involved in the practices of Egypt, losing sight of the promises given to the fathers. "Put away the gods which your fathers served on the other side of the River and *in Egypt*" (Joshua 24:14). "They shall no more offer their sacrifices to *demons*, after whom they have played the prostitute" (Leviticus 17:7). "They committed prostitution *in Egypt*, they committed prostitution in their youth" (Ezekiel 23:3). "But they rebelled against me and would not obey me. They did not cast away the abominations which were before their eyes, nor did they forsake *the idols of Egypt*" (Ezekiel 20:8).

Perhaps more than anything else the setting up of the golden calf at the foot of Sinai (Exodus 32) is the clearest indication of the inner heart inclination of the Israelites. Apart from divine intervention, they were no better than any other people. However, God did not give them the law in Egypt so that they might reform themselves and in some way earn their salvation. No; the covenant with Abraham still stood. Salvation was, as it has always been, by faith, not by works. He saved them and then gave them the law. Outwardly, all who passed through the Red Sea experienced the salvation of the LORD; but inwardly, only those who were true children of Abraham and who put their trust in the promise-word of the LORD were the recipients of eternal salvation.

But if in respect of spiritual fundamentals the situation at Sinai was the same as it had been with Abraham, why was there a Mosaic covenant at all? The time had arrived in terms of God's eternal counsel to manifest in visible form the eternal kingdom of God in the midst of a hostile world. "If you will indeed obey my voice and keep my covenant, you shall be my treasured possession among all peoples, for all the earth is mine; and you shall be to me a kingdom of priests and a holy nation" (Exodus 19:5-6). In a world living in alienation from God and opposition to him, Israel as the special, chosen people, were to fulfil their collective destiny by maintaining as a 'holy people' the standards of divine truth. As they lived lives in conformity with the norms that the LORD set before them, the promised line of 'offspring'/'seed' would be preserved until the climactic revelation in Jesus Christ. Israel as a nation, set apart in service to the LORD, would testify among the other nations of the world as to the standards of divine revelation and the reality of God's saving grace. They were to be a beacon of light in pagan darkness proclaiming God's purpose for mankind so that all nations might know why they existed and to whom they were answerable.

But Israel could not function in this way if they did not know God and what conduct he wished them to exhibit. Their acknowledgement of God in fealty and loyalty could only be expressed if they knew something of his character and wishes. It was one thing to recognise the fact of the LORD's action in saving them from Egypt. That would undoubtedly engender feelings of gratitude and the desire to respond appropriately to the one who had redeemed them. The motivation to respond was present and that was a healthy reaction. But it is quite another thing for the impulse to gratitude to be correctly translated into action. That requires knowledge. Exodus 32 shows us clearly what happens when gratitude displays itself without knowledge, or displays itself in defiance of knowledge. Moses is on the mountaintop, and down below the golden calf has been fabricated, and Aaron says , "These are your gods, O Israel, who brought you up out of the land of Egypt!" This was a gross caricature and deformation of the response of obedience and gratitude that was required. It was to avoid such a misconceived response that the law was given. The Israelites had been rescued from the spiritual darkness of Egypt as much as from the oppression and bondage of Egypt. The LORD at Sinai presented them with the standards of conduct he requires. He reeducated the family of promise. It became a nation with the promise. The people were taught how God wanted them to live so that they might fulfil their destiny. The Ten Commandments are part of the divine educational syllabus for the people of God.

The moral law

Now, if you like to probe and ask searching questions, you might at this point say to me, "Well, even accepting what you say regarding the Israelites at Sinai, there are still significant matters you have not established. I can see why you say that God had saved Israel, and that the Ten Commandments are part of God's instruction regarding the way in which their gratitude might be adequately structured. However, that does not show why the Ten Commandments are also for all people. How can they function as moral imperatives for the world in general?"

To answer that sort of question we need to note that the giving of the Ten Commandments at Sinai did not constitute the first revelation of God's requirements for human behaviour. Consider Genesis 26:5 where the LORD says to Isaac, "Abraham obeyed my voice and kept my charge, my commandments, my statutes, and my laws." Or again we might mention Exodus 16:28 where the LORD says to Moses regarding Israel, "How long will you refuse to keep my commandments and my laws?" Both texts relate to circumstances that existed before the Israelites came to Sinai, and both passages speak of commandments and laws as already existing. Critical scholars explain away these passages as confusion in the sources and a lapse from total consistency on the part of a later storyteller. But such explanations will not satisfy one who believes in the inspiration of Scripture and the authenticity of the narrative. The commandments and laws (in some sense) existed before Sinai.

To see how that could be we must begin our historical résumé earlier than the Fall of mankind. We need to consider the situation that prevailed in Eden. God created mankind in his image, after his likeness, so that they might have dominion over the realm he had willed into existence (Genesis 1:26). The terms 'image' and 'likeness' are not employed to indicate some physical resemblance between mankind and God. God is spirit, and any notion of corporeal similarity is quite misplaced in thinking about him. However, the Creator is the sovereign Lord of all that he made, and by constituting mankind in (or 'as') his image and likeness he delegated to them the right to rule over the created realm on his behalf. As the consummation of the creation process, mankind was divinely placed as God's representatives on earth with subordinate authority to ruler over the realm that he had made.

But while being made in (or as) the image and likeness of God indicated the role mankind was designated to fulfil on earth, their function of ruling as God's deputies also implies that they were divinely endowed so as to fulfil that role adequately and responsibly. God equipped mankind with a knowledge of what he wanted them to do and of how he required them to behave as ruling on his behalf over the world he had created. What has to be grasped is that, in terms of the moral and spiritual constitution of humanity, God gave knowledge of his will. He did not leave mankind in a vacuum or with an empty sheet as regards the policies and conduct that would please him. At creation such knowledge was impressed on the moral being and capacities of Adam and Eve. Perhaps we might more accurately say that such knowledge was 'concreated' with mankind. Human beings were created as answerable to God because there was implanted in the essence of their beings an inherent knowledge of how God wanted them to live and behave. That standard was not arbitrary, but reflected the character and disposition of God himself. He created mankind after his likeness to live and rule over his creation in a way that was patterned after the norms of heaven.

Of course, the situation that initially prevailed in Eden was lost at the Fall. But even though humanity has lost its original moral integrity, there can still be traced a remaining consciousness of those terms and standards with which mankind was endowed by God. There is a sense of right and wrong implanted within each one of us. We call it conscience, and it points back to the original constitution of unfallen mankind. It is to the operation of conscience that Paul refers when he says in Romans 2:14-15, "For when Gentiles, who do not have the law, by nature do what the law requires, they are a law to themselves, even though they do not have the law. They show that the work of the law is written on their hearts, while their conscience also bears witness, and their conflicting thoughts accuse or even excuse them." Now Paul uses the word 'law' in various ways, but here we see him saying that quite apart from the prescriptions of Sinai there is a sense in which law is written on the hearts even of those who had no direct knowledge of the revealed standards of the covenant community. He is affirming that conscience bears witness within each individual member of the human race to an inner awareness of moral standards.

However, mankind has fallen. Our moral faculties no longer operate flawlessly. While the testimony of conscience attests that there is a moral law, it cannot reliably or fully inform us as to what the requirements of that law are. We are influenced by the standards and practices of the society within which we live, and our moral perception is easily warped. Our own wrong desires can twist our understanding of what is right and wrong. Indeed the voice of conscience may be silenced by overexposure to malpractice or by the strength of corrupt desires within a person. Conscience, though real and perhaps active with uncomfortable frequency, is no longer a reliable guide as to what comprises the demands of God's moral law.

How, then, are we to ascertain what constitutes the moral law? At one level, instruction as to what God requires of mankind can be ascertained by reading the narratives of Scripture and drawing inferences from them. Genesis 1 and 2 describe specific duties and obligations placed on mankind before the Fall. Known as the Creation Ordinances, these include requirements such as to have offspring, to fill the earth and garner its resources, to live lives patterned after the divine paradigm of a seven-day cycle, to engage in work, and to have the family as the basic unit in society cemented in terms of the marriage bond. These ordinances were over and above the innate moral sensitivity with which Adam and Eve were endowed. In many respects they are applications of the moral law, or supplements to it. But their Edenic origin shows that they too are universal in their scope. Also, information regarding fundamental divine requirements may be found in the terms the LORD specified in the Noachic covenant (Genesis 9). Further, from specific incidents narrated in Genesis we can derive instruction regarding what type of conduct met with divine approval and what type did not.

Another approach to ascertaining the constituents of the moral law is presented in terms of natural law. This attempts to derive norms by a process of reasoning from what can be ascertained in the moral consciousness of mankind. We have already argued that the moral consciousness of mankind is no longer a reliable guide in such matters. Furthermore, natural law approaches to ethics are liable to fall into what is called the naturalistic fallacy. Namely, in arguing from what is perceived to exist, it is easy to attribute normativity to what exists. It is by no means the case that what is should be identified with what ought to be. Nonetheless, it is possible to modify a natural law approach into a form of creation ethics that starts from the infinite, personal God who willed all that is into existence and whose structure and purpose for his creation ought to be respected. Proceeding in this way may not be to enter a cul-de-sac.

However, the obvious Scriptural way to ascertain what constitutes the moral law is to consider what is found in the Ten Commandments. When the LORD took account of the moral and spiritual ignorance of the covenant people whom he had redeemed from Egypt, and when he considered the role he wished them to play in the furtherance of his covenant purposes, he did not leave them to establish the norms for their conduct by inference from what they knew of the past or by general reasoning from what they perceived of their own constitution. He was pleased to deal with the situation directly. He informed them once more of his moral law. It is summarily comprehended in the Ten Commandments, which are also known as the Decalogue.

Now, it can be confusing to equate precisely the moral law and the Decalogue, although we often use the Ten Commandments as theological shorthand for the moral law. It is more illuminating to speak of the Ten Commandments as an edition of the moral law. In saying that I do not suppose that the terms of the moral law are subject to change. The requirements of the moral law express the unchanging will of the Creator. But the expression of the moral law may vary. It was not the case that the Ten Commandments as recorded in Exodus were given in those precise words to Adam. However, the same set of principles was made known to him in terms suited to his circumstances. Furthermore, the Decalogue given at Sinai was an edition of the moral law conditioned by the stage then prevailing in the development of God's saving purposes (for example, in the reference to 'the land that the LORD your God is giving you', Exodus 20:12) and by the existing economic and social situation of the Israelites (for example, references

to male and female servants, and to oxen and donkeys, Exodus 20:
17). Interpretation of Scripture must make due allowance for such
developmental and cultural specifics present in the imperatives of the
Decalogue. But, being derived from the character of God himself,
the principles of moral law predate Sinai. They were revealed to
mankind at creation. Equally, the principles of the moral law postdate
Moses. However, there is now a fundamental difference. Neither the
Christian nor the non-Christian receives the moral law from the hand
of Moses, the mediator of the Sinai covenant. As we shall see, the
Christian receives the moral law from the hand of Christ, the mediator
of the new covenant, and the precepts of the law are reinforced by the
living example of Christ. For the non-Christian the moral law remains
as the standard the Creator requires of mankind.

That introduces another strand of thought. In writing to Timothy,
Paul said, "Now we know that the law is good, if one uses it lawfully,
understanding this, that the law is not laid down for the just but for the
lawless and disobedient, for the ungodly and sinners, for the unholy and
profane, for those who strike their fathers and mothers, for murderers,
the sexually immoral, men who practice homosexuality, enslavers,
liars, perjurers, and whatever else is contrary to sound doctrine, in
accordance with the glorious gospel of the blessed God with which I
have been entrusted" (1 Timothy 1:8-11). It might then be said, "Yes, I
can see the relevance of the moral law for the lawless and disobedient.
It sets before them the standards God the Creator requires of them.
But precisely how does that law relate to the believer? Does not Paul
say, 'the law is not laid down for the just'?"

One must not assume that there is only one purpose for the moral
law; that there is only one way in which it may be legitimately used.
Theology traditionally has set out a threefold distinction regarding the
use of the law.

There is *the civil or political use of the law*. It is given to restrain sin and to promote good conduct. In this it serves the purposes of common grace, preserving order in society while God works to bring to completion his saving purpose for his church.

There is *the pedagogic use of the law*. The law brings individuals under conviction of sin, and convinces them of their inability to meet the demands of the law. The law teaches or instructs ('pedagogy'). It serves to show need for redemption. The law is "our schoolmaster to bring us unto Christ, that we might be justified by faith" (Galatians 3: 24 – Authorised Version).

There is *the didactic or normative use of the law*, often termed the third use of the law, in which it functions as the rule of life for believers. Lutherans stress the second use of the law. In their thinking the third use of the law exists only because of remaining sin in a believer. Since that is being progressively eliminated, they consider that the didactic function of the law is of only transient significance. However, Reformed thinkers accord a far greater role to the third use of the law. They see it as providing a rule of life which informs and shapes the gratitude of those who have been saved. It is, then, primarily in terms of that third use of the law that the moral law impinges on the life of the believer.

The Decalogue and the rest of the Mosaic Law

There are a great many serious-minded, thinking Christians who have difficulty with identifying the Ten Commandments as the moral law and with accepting that the Commandments have on-going validity. They bring forward a number of arguments to support their position, some of them based on what is said in the New Testament. I will consider these later. But there is one argument, derived from the Old Testament, which ought to be considered here. It is an argument that seems plausible. It denies that there is any exegetical warrant for dividing up the various requirements of the Mosaic covenant, and asserts that the Ten Commandments no longer apply because the New Testament teaches that believers are no longer under the law of Moses. It is pointed out that Paul wrote in Galatians 3:29, "If you are Christ's, then you are Abraham's offspring, heirs according to promise", and not "… then you are Moses' offspring, bound to the law". This being so, it is contended that it is illegitimate to curtail the freedom of the believer by exempting one aspect of the Mosaic Law from abrogation. The fundamental fallacy is identified as the introduction into the Old Testament of an unwarranted division within the requirements of the Mosaic Law. God did not just give the Ten Commandments to the Israelites; he gave the whole of the Mosaic Law. No Israelite was ever free to say, "I will abide by these Ten Commandments, but as for that sacrificial, ritual, ceremonial or judicial law, I will not be regulated by it." The Mosaic covenant was a unity, and the law that expressed its demands was a unity. So, it is argued, obedience to the Mosaic covenant had to be total; there were no optional requirements in it. In its entirety it has been done away with in Christ. Therefore, it is hermeneutically flawed to isolate one part of the integral structure of the law, label it the moral law, and argue that it alone is exempt from obsolescence.

I am not sure that I agree with the presupposition that it is illegitimate to read from the New Testament back into the Old. I find that there are, for instance, many Messianic promises in the Old Testament that can only be adequately understood in the light of their fulfilment. But leaving that aside, I would wish to argue that right from the start the Israelites knew there was something distinctive about the Ten Commandments. It is the evident testimony of Scripture that they had a different status from the other regulations of the Mosaic covenant.

- First of all, they were delivered in a special way—spoken immediately by the voice of God (Exodus 20:18-19; Deuteronomy 5:4; 18:16), whereas the others were communicated privately to Moses and then announced by him to the people. The theophanic display of the majesty and greatness of the LORD seems to have been reserved for the deliverance of these Commandments.
- Also, their number, ten, is a symbol of completeness. Much of what is written regarding Scriptural numerics is fanciful and incapable of proof, but in all that has been established as certain we find the symbolic import of ten as being completeness. 'Ten' signifies a definite whole, in which nothing is lacking, and this marks the Commandments as having a unity that

requires them to be considered together.

- The Commandments were written by the finger of God on two tables of stone—on both sides (Exodus. 31:18; 32:15-16). There was no room for future additions to what had been written, and the use of stone pointed to the lasting and imperishable nature of what had to be preserved.
- The Commandments were laid up inside the Tabernacle, the divinely commissioned structure that was to be the focus of the divine presence as he dwelled in the midst of his people. Indeed, the stone tablets, known as 'the testimony', were placed in the box-like receptacle known as the ark (Exodus 25: 16; 40:20), and the ark itself was covered over by the Mercy Seat or the Cover of Propitiation. The status accorded the Commandments was completely revealed when in the inmost chamber of the Tabernacle the LORD was pleased to presence himself over the ark within which lay the tablets of the law.

We must also notice how this fits in with the prevailing practice in ancient Near Eastern treaty arrangements which were the literary form the LORD condescended to use in setting out his covenant prescriptions for his people. In these documents, the overlord or Great King first set out the general terms and policy he expected his subject people to follow, and then he enumerated the detailed stipulations they were to observe. This sequence of general requirements followed by detailed stipulations matches precisely the sequence of Ten Commandments followed by the other aspects of the Mosaic Law. (Indeed there are scholars who argue that in the book of Deuteronomy the material is thematically ordered first by the basic stipulations of Deuteronomy 5 followed by elaboration and application of them in chapters 6–26.) The order of the covenant prescriptions was, therefore, one that the Israelites at Sinai would have been able to understand against the prevailing usage of the times. The LORD first set before his covenant people the policy he wished to impose on their life as the basic value structure and goals of the community. Then he delivered the specific procedures by which that policy could be worked out in their particular culture and environment.

In fact the Old Testament term is not the Ten Commandments, but "the words of the covenant, the ten words" (Exodus 34:28). That is why Decalogue, literally 'ten words', is arguably a better term. While they are commandments, they are not 'law' in our narrower, modern sense. There are no penalties stated. What human tribunal would ever be able to enforce "Thou shalt not covet"? These are the words of the covenant king, setting out his stipulations that are the essential features of the moral law.

The Decalogue represents the fundamental principles of divine direction for human living; this is God's policy document. As such it corresponds to the policy that God originally enunciated to Adam. What God requires from mankind is not arbitrary. It flows from the essential nature of what God is in himself and, therefore, what he requires and expects from those he has created in his image and likeness. Because it is a reflection of the divine nature, it does not change. There is not one policy for human behaviour before the Fall and another afterwards, though the extent to which any individual may achieve that standard has inevitably changed. The potential of the human race for obedience has been corrupted and undermined, but the standard remains the same. The ideal is not departed from, and it is the same ideal that the LORD presented to Israel at Sinai in a way in which they would readily have appreciated the difference between the fundamental principles stated and the subordinate regulations that applied those principles in a more detailed way.

The application of the other laws

In the Decalogue we have God's policy prescriptions for human behaviour. These are the essential principles which are to inform human conduct and also the conduct of his people. But the principles themselves are very general statements. These goals have to be translated into far more specific policies if we are to implement them in daily life. One way to move from the general terms of the Decalogue to more particular moral norms is to proceed by logical deduction, that is, by ascertaining what may be validly inferred from the general statements. For instance, if a duty is commanded, then the opposite behaviour may be taken as forbidden. If one type of conduct is commended, then similar actions will also be approved. In this way a comprehensive set of moral norms might be validly established.

However, God went further than leaving the ancient Israelites to bring logic to bear on the general principles he had given them. He also provided them with authoritative examples worked for their particular environment and circumstances. The examples were not comprehensive; not every aspect of the life of the community was covered. Some areas were dealt with in greater detail than others. But God, in essence, said to Israel, "This is the way you are to live as my people."

These specific directives are to be found throughout the books of Exodus, Leviticus, Numbers, and Deuteronomy, and they contain divine instruction for the Israelites of old and for future generations as well. But the way in which the other Mosaic laws still function has been a matter of considerable controversy in Reformed circles in recent years. I do not want to give a blow-by-blow account of what has been said, but simply to indicate a way of approaching the matter that I believe is helpful.

Because we are not living in the same cultural or sociological environment as ancient Israel and, more especially, because we are not living at the same stage in the unfolding of the divine plan of salvation, we may not simply take the other laws and say they apply still. The Church in the post New Testament era operates in a more mature environment. The injunctions and examples of old are to be thought through and their general principles applied.

Let us begin with one simple instance about which there is general agreement. The laws concerning sacrifice, the festivals, the priesthood and the sanctuary. They were designed to teach Israel about the atoning work of the Great High Priest who would come. They are not discarded by Christ but fulfilled by and in him. They are no longer applicable. It is not that they are devoid of teaching, but rather we are to appreciate this is how God taught his people when they were in the equivalent of the primary or elementary class at school. It is still profitable to trace out the pattern of Christ and his work in the ordinances of old.

Then there are the food and dietary obligations. These were decisively set aside by Christ (Mark 7:19). Many of these regulations did not directly involve abiding ethical principles. This can be clearly seen in Deuteronomy 14:21, "You shall not eat anything that has died naturally. You may give it to the sojourner who is within your towns, that he may eat it, or you may sell it to a foreigner. For you are a people holy to the LORD your God." Israel was permitted to give or sell such food to aliens and foreigners, an odd qualification if eating such things was morally wrong. Rather it was the case that certain special regulations applied to Israel that did not apply to other people. Many of the restrictions that were imposed on them were designed to remind them of their special status as a people consecrated to God.

The same applies to restrictions such as, "You shall not wear cloth of wool and linen mixed together. You shall make yourself tassels on the four corners of the garment with which you cover yourself" (Deuteronomy 22:12). I don't think it is totally flippant to say that is almost equivalent to a requirement to wear school uniform. Every day when they got dressed and ventured into the wider community, the Israelites were reminded that they stood apart from the world around them. Thus, they were instructed to identify with one another as a community with shared practices that pointed to their common dedication to the LORD. Although the 'childish' way in which the duty was presented to them has passed away, there is a basic principle that still applies. The people of God should not be conformed to the way of the world, but transformed into those who are spiritually different in the way God wants. "What fellowship has light with darkness? What accord has Christ with Belial? Or what portion does a believer share with an unbeliever? … Go out from their midst, and be separate from them" (2 Corinthians 6:14-15, 17). It is not now a matter of outward signs and symbols or outward restrictions, but of inner heart dedication evidenced in God-honouring living.

What procedure is followed in that example just given? As we look at any particular injunction of the Old Testament law, we are to ask what principle is involved in this requirement. What aspect of the Decalogue was God teaching the Israelites about? What spiritual truth received particular embodiment in this legislation? Then we ask how that general principle applies now: not just now in terms of our culture and society, but in terms of where we are located after the death and resurrection of

Jesus. Various authors use different terms to describe this process of inference. The Westminster Confession talked about the general equity of the law[2], meaning the law maker's intention in giving them. Others talk about deriving intermediate axioms from the Old Testament laws. Others present the approach in terms of derived moral principles. Care must be taken not to absolutise these intermediate principles. Authority does not inhere in them. Rather, it lies in the Scriptures from which they are drawn. The derived principles are the product of the sanctified reflection of God's people on his revelation, but here on earth the sanctified are not yet glorified. Because we are not yet made perfect in holiness, there is always the possibility of error, and especially there is the possibility of incompleteness. New circumstances may arise regarding in which the previous formulation of the underlying paradigm is less than adequate. So these axioms have to be constantly subjected to scrutiny and potential revision in the light of the biblical text itself.

This is the sort of process Paul himself set out. In 1 Corinthians 9: 9 he cited Deuteronomy 25:4 ("Do not muzzle an ox while it is treading out the grain") in defending his right to receive material support from the Corinthians. It is not a ceremonial law as such, but pertains more to the socio-political laws that were to govern Israel's behaviour in ordinary life. Paul was not contending that the maintenance of gospel preachers was directly in view in Deuteronomy, but that there is a basic principle involved in the law namely, that effort is to be appropriately rewarded. As the underlying principle can be applied to situations other than that of its initial setting, the apostle was warranted in using this law paradigmatically or analogically. The particular example illustrated a general principle which itself was an application of the eighth commandment, "You shall not steal" (Exodus 20:15).

Consider also the well-known example of Deuteronomy 22:8. "When you build a new house, you shall make a parapet for your roof, that you may not bring the guilt of blood upon your house, if anyone should fall from it." I have heard a story that one of the spokesmen for theonomy (which argues for the abiding validity of the law in all its detail) was once challenged regarding this law. He was asked, "Does the roof of your house have a parapet round it?" He was forced to concede that it had not. However, he added, "But my outdoor swimming pool has a fence round it." In saying that he effectively undermined his whole point of view. He was no longer arguing for the abiding validity of the law in all its detail (that would have required a parapet round his roof). However, he had quite properly asked what is the principle that lies behind this law. It is an application of the sixth commandment, "You shall not commit murder" (Exodus 20:13). The roof tops of houses in Palestine were used in evenings as places to have a meal and to meet with family and friends. Whoever built a house had to give consideration to the future safety of others who might inadvertently slip and fall. This might well provide a Scriptural basis for building control regulations. It was certainly the case that putting a safety fence round a swimming pool was complying with the underlying principle of the law, while at the same time setting to one side the detail of the Old Testament regulation.

Or again, one might think of Leviticus 19:36, "You shall have just balances, just weights, a just ephah and a just hin." That could be taken as the Biblical basis for weights and standards regulations and for trading standards legislation in general. It again applies the stipulation of the moral law, "You shall not steal", in the realm of the market place.

One might also reflect on the injunction not to charge interest on loans: "You shall not charge interest on loans to your brother, interest on money, interest on food, interest on anything that is lent for interest. You may charge a foreigner interest, but you may not charge your brother interest" (Deuteronomy 23:19-20). Again the fact that interest could be charged to a foreigner shows that there is no absolute moral prohibition here. Also we have to read that command in the context of a world where economic advance was limited. Modern business corporations did not exist nor were there elaborate financial institutions. What sort of loan was being asked for? One to enable another person and his family to survive. What was being forbidden? The exploitation of one who had fallen on hard times. Such counsel regarding the economically disadvantaged may well have implications for loans and aid given to third world countries.

Other passages present greater challenges to the expositor. I have already mentioned Deuteronomy 14:21 and the regulation about animals that have fallen down dead. But the verse ends, "You shall not boil a young goat in its mother's milk". That is also found in Exodus 23:19. It forms the basis in Jewish dietary law for not eating meat and dairy products simultaneously. Of the many attempts to explain what is involved here the most probable is that which sees it as a rejection of Canaanite practice, which is illustrated in a tablet from Ugarit which describes "boiling a kid in milk, a lamb in butter" as part of the ceremonies associated with agricultural festivals. Although it does not specifically talk of its mother's milk, it may be that the element of heartless cruelty involved in cooking the young animal in the milk that should have sustained it made it especially objectionable. At any rate the fact that Israel were commanded not to follow such a pagan practice would reinforce their distinctive lifestyle as the LORD's covenant people.

There is still guidance to be derived from the specific examples of the divinely given applications of God's requirements to Israel. This was the way in which God showed how the fundamental principles of the moral law could be applied in a variety of circumstances faced by Israel of old. The Church today is no longer presented with such a detailed set of regulations, but careful scrutiny of the divinely given paradigms still provides guidance as to how to move from general principles to application in particular situations.

The law as a covenant of works

We have already remarked that the law was not given to Israel in Egypt so that they might earn their salvation by obedience. That would have been salvation by works-righteousness. But even so there are passages such as Leviticus 18:5, "You shall therefore keep my statutes and my rules; if a person does them, he shall live by them: I am the LORD", which have perplexed many because they point to an element of reward for obedience being at the core of the Mosaic covenant.

When the moral law was given to Adam in innocence, it was given in terms of the covenant of works. Adam was created sinless, yet able to be tempted. If he obeyed God for a limited period and did not yield to temptation, he would have had conferred on him incorruptibility, which would have made him fit to appear in God's presence in heaven. The created order was not a static realm. It had a dynamic. Through obedience there was a pathway to confirmed life and uninterrupted fellowship with God in his eternal kingdom. There was the possibility of works-righteousness for Adam in that the reward of eternal life would have been his on the basis of his unblemished adherence to the moral law.

However, when the moral law was reissued to Israel at Sinai, it was not a return to the original covenant of works. There was no possibility of Israel meriting eternal salvation by obedience. There is a legal, works-righteousness aspect to the Mosaic covenant, but it does not relate to individual eternal salvation. The inauguration of the Mosaic covenant did not supersede God's previous gracious provision formalised in the Abrahamic covenant. It remained the case that the final destiny of each individual was determined by a response of faith to the promise of God. It was a matter of faith, not of works. But the specific role accorded Israel in the divine purpose of salvation was to be a holy nation, and in terms of that the Mosaic Law code was given so that their life as a nation might typify the life of the age to come in fellowship with God. Living by that standard they epitomised the life of harmony that would prevail in heavenly bliss.

It is not enough to say that the Sinai covenant was a temporal covenant merely concerned with Israel's enjoyment of the occupation of the land and the good things that went along with that. Like so much else in the Mosaic dispensation, occupation of the land was symbolic of Scriptural truth yet to be revealed in actuality. Those who would live in fellowship with God as loyal subjects of his kingdom are to mirror his character and conduct. "You shall be holy, for I the LORD your God am holy" (Leviticus 19:1).

Because God's plan of redemption was not finally fulfilled in the time of Moses, truth about it could not be stated in relation to the facts of its consummation. Instead the message of salvation was centred about symbols and types that indirectly pointed to the truth, but were not themselves the final reality. They were divinely instituted and mandated to point forward to the ultimate revelation in Christ Jesus.

The law was given to Israel because in her role of manifesting heaven (or the age to come) on earth she must also make clear that holiness and heaven go hand in hand. Likewise when God prospered his people who kept his holy law it was to prove that heaven would be a place of happiness and blessedness. When Israel became indifferent to

God's law and followed idols, the nation forfeited its unique privileges and was expelled from the land flowing with milk and honey.

God in effect promised Israel that if as a kingdom of priests and a holy nation it kept the law he had enjoined on it, he would reward it with great temporal prosperity. This agreement thus took the form of works-righteousness. It is better to avoid saying that it took the form of a covenant of works because there are such decided differences. Nonetheless, Israel had voluntarily undertaken to fulfil the law, and if she did, she would enjoy the blessings of the land, that is, in terms of Leviticus 18:5 "live" as a nation in the land, enjoying its provision. But the Israelites were never given to understand that this agreement had anything to do with their individual eternal standing before God. They were never taught to think that by fulfilling any aspect of the law they were circumventing the Abrahamic covenant and earning eternal life. Every believing Israelite was aware — repeatedly and vividly made aware by the sacrificial ordinances — that his eternal salvation depended on the atoning provision that was made graciously and sovereignly by the LORD.

Jesus and the law

So far we have mainly looked at the role of law in the Old Testament, albeit we have done so with New Testament spectacles on. However, an Old Testament orientation frequently leaves people saying in effect, "But I am not an Israelite at the foot of Sinai. I am a Christian living after the death and resurrection of Jesus Christ. What has that whole dispensation of law to do with my present situation?" I trust that many aspects of the answer to such a question are already evident, and that they will become even more so as we come to examine what the New Testament says about the law.

It is indeed remarkable how much of the New Testament is taken up with the relationship between it and the Old Testament. The place of the law is not something that is confined to the periphery of New Testament teaching. It is a theme that recurs through gospels and epistles alike. For converted Jews it was a matter of intense interest to ascertain how the divine plan of salvation had progressed and how in the changed conditions their relationship to the law of God had been altered by their new allegiance to Christ. For the Gentile convert who on coming to Christ was presented with the Scriptures of the Old Testament as the word of God, it was equally vital to know, "How does all this relate to me?" So the problem we have to grapple with is not the sparsity of relevant New Testament evidence regarding the law, but the abundance of it. We can only consider some of the texts that are involved in the matter. Even so, I hope to be able to bring out what I consider to be the principal elements of New Testament teaching on the matter. Let us look first at the gospels and what we are told about Jesus' attitude to the law.

In fact the word 'law' is used very rarely in the gospels. It does not occur at all in Mark; in Matthew it is found eight times and in Luke nine times, mainly to describe the Pentateuch, the five books of Moses. In Jesus' teaching — indeed, throughout the New Testament — the word 'law' is used in a variety of ways. In Matthew 11:13 Jesus says that the Law and the Prophets prophesied until John, that is, they authoritatively declared God's word. Here 'Law', as distinguished from the Prophets (and so spelled with a capital letter), indicates the revelation given through Moses. Its significance is not so much 'law' as command, but rather, reflecting the Jewish use of the term as divine instruction, it is 'Law' as revelation, as Scripture. It sums up the whole covenantal disposition that had been instituted by Moses. But a new era dawned with the coming of John; the time of Messianic salvation had arrived. In this new order the relationship between God and his people is no longer mediated through the terms of the Mosaic covenant, but through Jesus himself. The whole of the Old Testament revelation was divinely directed towards him and found its fulfilment in him. In this way divine law and commandment, the controlling influence of the Old Testament word of divine revelation and command, are everywhere present in Jesus' teaching.

It is possible to trace this influence by looking first at the end of Jesus' earthly ministry when he addressed his disciples and commissioned them for the work they were to do. He said, "All authority in heaven and on earth has been given to me. Go therefore and make disciples of all nations, ... teaching them to observe all that

I have commanded you" (Matthew 28:18-20). We firstly notice the assertion of absolute authority. 'Therefore' creates the bridge between the Lord's authority and the task facing his Church. Not only do they go in his name to evangelise, but they are also directed to teach those who are converts. The Church's teaching is to comprise the totality of the Lord's commands.

What commands, then, did Jesus give to his disciples? The Sermon on the Mount (Matthew 5–7) is his major address on the ethics of the kingdom of heaven inaugurated by his coming. This sermon, too, is pervaded by the authority with which Jesus speaks and by which he sets out the standards that are to prevail. "The crowds were astonished at his teaching, for he was teaching them as one who had authority, and not as their scribes" (Matthew 7:28-29). His preaching was in sharp contrast to the mode employed by the Jewish rabbis who buttressed every tenet of their teaching with citations of the sayings of earlier rabbis. Jesus deliberately avoided that technique. "You have heard that it was said to those of old" (Matthew 5: 21, 33) refers not to what Moses said, but to the teachings of the rabbis, over against which Jesus set, "But I say to you" (Matthew 5:22, 34). He spoke with an authority that exceeded that of the rabbis. Indeed, he also avoided the prophetic formulation, "Thus says the LORD". Instead Jesus said, "But I say unto you", or "Truly, truly (Amen, Amen, an asseveration that complete trust and reliance could be placed in what followed) I say unto you" (John 3:3; *cf.* Matthew 5:18), in which uniquely he brought the Amen to the beginning of what he had to say, rather than using it as a response of acceptance at the close of what another said. Jesus spoke with authority and originality.

In his teaching Jesus showed that he possessed an authority equal to that of the Law; indeed an authority that is above the Law. But he did not use that authority to set aside the Law. Matthew 5:17-20 is the key passage for determining Jesus' attitude towards the Law. He begins by saying, "Do not think that I have come to abolish the Law or the Prophets; I have not come to abolish them but to fulfil them" (Matthew 5:17). There have been many disputes over the nature of the contrast indicated by the words 'abolish' and 'fulfil'. Though it is undoubtedly true that Jesus personally kept the Law, the idea expressed here does not seem to be that of 'abolish' as indicating personal flouting of adherence to the standards of the Law and 'fulfil' as compliance with its demands. 'Abolish' would point to the abrogation and termination of the Law. Jesus emphatically denies that is his intention. Instead he would 'fulfil' the Law. Undoubtedly that involved validating and confirming the Law, but more is conveyed by 'fulfil' than the static maintenance of existing standards as they had always been. There is progression and consummation. Jesus brought the Law forward to its full intent and proper expression. He did not disparage it. He ensured that it came to perfect realisation.

How did he do that? 'I have come' (Matthew 5:17) points to the messianic mission of Jesus. And, with his arrival, it was inevitable that those aspects of the Mosaic Law which had been instituted as part of Israel's role until the coming of the Messiah were put into honourable retirement. They had served their God-given purpose and were now "obsolete and growing old" (Hebrews 8:13). When Jesus declared that a person could not be defiled by food (Mark 7:15), he thereby declared all food clean (Mark 7:19). In this he brought to an end the ceremonial law. But supremely, by offering himself as the sacrifice for sin, Jesus superseded the Levitical priests of the Mosaic dispensation and also, once for all, presented the final sacrifice that obtained eternal redemption (Hebrews 8:12), thus bringing the worship of the Temple to an end. It was not that these regulations were annulled, but consummated. What they had foreshadowed had now arrived.

But there was more to the Mosaic Law than the observation of rites and ceremonies, of sacrifices, feasts, and food laws. There were also laws regarding human conduct, in particular the moral law of the Decalogue. "I tell you the truth, until heaven and earth disappear, not the smallest letter, not the least stroke of a pen, will by any means disappear from the Law until everything is accomplished" (Matthew 5:18, NIV). Jesus here shows his concern for the detail of the Law. Such an attitude is often misunderstood as legalism, as a dead orthodoxy focusing on the minutiae of credal or ritual observance and satisfied with stereotyped expression and ossified forms. As this passage clearly shows, Jesus combined scathing hostility towards the rigid externality of the religious groups of his day with total regard for all the implications of what God had laid down. The details were of significance and not to be set aside. "Therefore whoever relaxes one of the least of these commandments and teaches others to do the same will be called least in the kingdom of heaven, but whoever does them and teaches them will be called great in the kingdom of heaven" (Matthew 5:19).

Even more significant in Jesus' presentation of the law is his insistence that the demands of the kingdom of heaven are greater than the outward show of conformity to the standards of the law promoted by the teachers of the law and practised by the Pharisees. In Matthew 5:21-48 Jesus illustrates his teaching with six examples in which he contrasts what he says, not with the law as given by Moses, but with the law as presented in a superficial fashion to past and present generations by the religious teachers of the Jews. Jesus does not just forbid the overt act of murder or that of adultery, but also the inner feelings and thought processes that may precipitate the outward action. The anger that leads to murder and the lustful desire that leads to adultery are shown to be the source of misconduct and condemned along with it. It is true that the need for appropriate inner motivation had always been recognised. After all, the tenth commandment says, "You shall not covet" (Exodus 20:17). But the stress on the sweeping implications of such heart disposition is characteristic of Jesus' moral teaching. Being a citizen of the kingdom of heaven requires inner conformity to the demands of the law.

Jesus did not set aside the moral law. Far from it; he warned against diluting any of the least of its commands (Matthew 5:19). He rejected the scribal interpretation of the law, which the Jews of his day considered to be an intrinsic part of the law. When the rich man wanted to know how to inherit eternal life, Jesus pointed him to the Decalogue, quoting six of its commands and thus upholding its continuing relevance (Mark 10:17-19). In effect he says these are an abiding revelation of what right conduct and goodness involve. These are God's standards; they are still valid.

The gospel records show conclusively that Jesus regarded the Old Testament as the inspired Word of God, and the law as the divinely given rule of life. What is more, he did not just urge others to obey the injunctions of the law; he did so himself. Those who disparage the moral law should remember that Christ lived perfectly in accordance with it. Those who would truly be his disciples must recognise and adopt the standards by which he lived. It is one of the supreme privileges of the New Testament era that we see the law not only revealed and commanded as at Sinai, but revealed and perfectly lived out in Jesus Christ. It is not just a matter of precept, but also a matter of living example.

The law and love

There is one aspect of Christ's teaching that still has to be examined, namely the relationship between law and love. The question is often posed, "If love is the fulfilment of the law, then do Christians still need the law?"

In line with his consistent teaching regarding the significance of correct inner motivation in meeting the demands of the law, Jesus preeminently emphasised the significance of love. In the disputes that took place in the Temple precincts shortly before his death, he was asked by a teacher of the law which of the commandments was the greatest. Jesus replied, "You shall love the Lord your God with all your heart and with all your soul and with all your mind. This is the great and first commandment. And a second is like it: You shall love your neighbour as yourself. On these two commandments depend all the Law and the Prophets" (Matthew 22:37-40). We notice here that Jesus did not reject the question as basically flawed. There are greater and lesser matters in the law. Elsewhere Jesus criticised the teachers of the law and the Pharisees for having "neglected the weightier matters of the law: justice and mercy and faithfulness" (Matthew 23:23). But that was not to condone an attitude of indifference to certain aspects of the law, for he added, "These you ought to have done, without neglecting the others." Equally we see here that Jesus maintained his respect for the Old Testament and did not try to subvert its authority. As the two fundamental principles of the law, he quotes two Old Testament passages, Deuteronomy 6:5 and Leviticus 19:18. It is right to be suspicious of any teaching that seeks to drive a wedge between our Lord's attitude to the law and that which should characterise those who follow him.

Jesus points to the role that love plays in the life of the citizen of the kingdom of heaven. He demands love with an exclusiveness that means that all other commands lead up to it, and all righteousness finds its norm in it. "If you love me, you will keep my commandments" (John 14:15). "Whoever has my commandments and keeps them, he it is who loves me" (John 14:21). Love evidences itself by keeping Christ's commandments, and those commandments are to be principally located in the moral law which expresses God's will for mankind.

There was a well-known and long-running series of television advertisements where a variety of storylines were used to present essentially the same plot. The hero carried out some feat of derring-do — climbing mountains, abseiling down precipices, or what ever — to find his beloved and present her with his gift of a box of chocolates. The feats of endurance and bravery that he carried out testified to the intensity of his devotion, but they would have been profitless without information about the likes and dislikes of the one he sought to please. What if her preference was for a different brand of chocolates? What if she had gone on a diet and had forsworn chocolate?

In the same way the citizen of the kingdom has totally and unequivocally surrendered his or her life to Jesus Christ. Faith's grasp of what has been done by Christ as Saviour leads to a love responsive to the supreme display of love. "In this is love, not that we have loved God but that he loved us and sent his Son to be the propitiation for our sins" (1 John 4:10). "We love because he first loved us" (1 John 4:19). Divine love evokes love, and the love of the faithful seeks to express itself in action, but that action to be acceptable has to be informed by knowledge. John Murray summed the matter up in a dictum that he expressed in a number of ways: "Love does not excogitate its own norm".[3] Love requires information about the preferences and desires of the one who is loved. Love towards God requires that attention be paid to the directions he has given about what pleases him.

Love involves basing one's whole being in God, committing oneself to him with unreserved confidence and leaving with him all care and final responsibility. This new inner orientation arouses emotional attachment and resolution of one's will to please God. Real obedience to God and Christ is nothing more and nothing less than the exercise of love and the directing of it to what God has commanded. Strictly speaking, there is no ground for the distinction commonly made of internal and external obedience: all true obedience is internal, consisting in the exercise of love, and external obedience is simply the expression of the inner disposition of the heart.

There are many today who articulate a theology of love that they set over against law. They dismiss law and say that love is the only criterion we need to employ. Now, if ever there was an individual who might be reckoned competent to live on the basis of love quite apart from law, that individual was Christ himself. But what testimony does he bear regarding himself? "For I have not spoken on my own authority, but the Father who sent me has himself given me a commandment—what to say and what to speak. And I know that his commandment is eternal life. What I say, therefore, I say as the Father has told me" (John 12:49-50). Just as Jesus lived out a life of love informed by his knowledge of the Father's commandment given to him, so those who follow him are called on to express their love in the same way. "This is the love of God, that we keep his commandments"

(1 John 5:3). The core values of God's Old Testament revelation, the moral law, are not set aside but reinforced, and it is made absolutely clear that it is only in a spirit of love that the divine norms of the moral law can properly be observed.

Paul and the law

Having looked at Jesus' view of the law, we now turn to the other major body of New Testament teaching regarding law, namely that found in the writings of the apostle Paul. While there is no contradiction between the teaching of Jesus and that of Paul as regards the law, it must be acknowledged that their presentation is significantly different. For instance, it is not surprising that reading Paul's epistles has led some to conclude that he viewed the law as utterly obsolete and defunct, to the extent that the Christian no longer has anything to do with it. In Romans 7:6 Paul wrote, "But now we are released from the law, having died to that which held us captive, so that we serve not under the old written code but in the new life of the Spirit." Has the Spirit-led life replaced the old written law code so that it no longer has a place in the life of the believer, who has in effect died in relation to the law? In Romans 10:4 Paul says, "Christ is the end of the law for righteousness to everyone who believes", and there are those who argue that by this Paul means that the role of the law in God's saving purposes has ended absolutely with the coming of Christ. Indeed, it is contended that the law has reached its terminus as far as providing guidance for the conduct of the believer, for Paul also urges the church at Rome: "Owe no one anything, except to love each other, for the one who loves another has fulfilled the law" (Romans 13:8). In place of a life regulated by the law of God, Paul's message, it is claimed, presents Christians as simply controlled by love and informed by the Spirit as to how to behave.

Undoubtedly there are many passages in which Paul writes negatively concerning the law, but that is not the whole of his message. It is necessary to get a balanced overview of his teaching. Paul uses the Greek word for 'law' some 119 times. He sometimes uses it to refer to the Old Testament Scriptures (*e.g.* in "the Law and the Prophets", Romans 3:21); sometimes as a general principle of action (*e.g.* "the law of my mind ... the law of sin", Romans 7:23); but most often what he has in mind is the whole system instituted for Israel in the Sinai covenant. Paul never uses the word 'law' in the plural. He characteristically thinks of law as a unity, as a comprehensive totality in which the parameters of conduct are set out. He certainly did not try to demonstrate the superiority of specific Mosaic enactments by comparing them with the legislation of other nations. What he was concerned to analyse was the impact of the Mosaic covenant on the Judaism of his day. It is law in the complex unity of the ordinances of Sinai that Paul had in mind when he said that "the law came in" (Romans. 5:20) or that "it was added" (Galatians 3:19). Possession of the law was the privilege accorded to Israel after the Exodus, and it had continued to mark off the Jews from the rest of the world.

A number of times Paul uses the phrase "works of the law" or simply "works" to denote observance of what the law demanded. The apostle had no doubt that "by works of the law no one will be justified" (Galatians 2:16; *cf.* also Romans 3:20, 28). Indeed, "all who rely on works of the law are under a curse" (Galatians 3:10). What Paul meant by this has been debated in much recent scholarship on Paul, with many arguing that the expression "works of the law" does not refer to the moral law or to the Mosaic ordinances in general, but specifically to compliance with those ordinances that gave the Jews their particular identity by marking them off from other nations — circumcision, the food laws and the observance of holy days. They argue that Paul's vision of the gospel encompassed all nations and could not tolerate such nationalistic barriers that blocked the inclusion of other peoples. Paul opposed the notion that to become a Christian one had first to become a Jew, and so he expressed himself in sweeping negatives against those who advocated such a message.

However, limiting Paul's message to a condemnation of these national identity markers is to conceive of his thinking in far too narrow a fashion. As traditional Reformed exegesis correctly brings out, Paul's point concerns the whole of mankind. In Galatians 3:10 he does not focus simply on the Jews. He makes a point that is valid for "all" without exception. He opposes and condemns a legalistic conception of life wherever it is found. Why? Because such a view promotes the idea that acceptance with God can be earned by observance of the law. Such works-righteousness was emphatically not what Abraham achieved. Rather, on the basis of his faith in God's word he was given a right standing before God and entered into possession of the promises of the covenant (Romans 4). So to think that salvation can be obtained on the basis of human merit is at utter variance with the gospel of Christ. "You are severed from Christ, you who would be justified by the law; you have fallen away from grace" (Galatians 5:4).

Though Paul decisively rejects observance of the law as the basis of salvation, he does not on that account disparage the law. He has no doubt that "the law is holy, and the commandment is holy and righteous and good" (Romans 7:12). Its standards were absolute and pure, and it had been given by God to act as "guardian" (Galatians 3:24) until the gospel was revealed in its fulness in Christ. The problem with the law was not some deficiency in its standards, but in human inability to keep those standards. "If a law had been given that could give life, then righteousness would indeed be by the law" (Galatians 3:21). However, the verdict that must be reached is that achieving righteousness in that way is foreclosed for fallen humanity. "By works of the law no human being will be justified in his sight … all have sinned and fall short of the glory of God" (Romans 3:20, 23). Theoretically law observance appears to be a possible route to heaven; but in reality, because of sin, it is a closed road for fallen humanity. The law can no longer provide for any person access to God. We have not kept, do not keep, and cannot keep the law.

But Paul's message is not primarily a critique of Jewish misunderstandings of what God had revealed to them. It is a presentation of the gospel. The ministry of Jesus Christ has brought the previous administration of God to an end and has inaugurated "a new creation. The old has passed away; behold, the new has come" (2 Corinthians 5:17). When Paul speaks of the believer not being under law ("you are not under law but under grace", Romans 6:14), he is primarily saying that the believer is no longer living under the Mosaic dispensation. Those who through faith put their trust in the divine promise have a radically different standing before God. It is totally dependent upon and achieved in and through Jesus Christ. He is the one who died for the ungodly, and who has procured for them the gift of righteousness. "As by one man's disobedience the many were made sinners, so by the one man's obedience the many will be made righteous" (Romans 5:19). But where does this free gift of righteousness and justification leave the believer in relation to the moral law of God?

In Romans 10:4 Paul says, "Christ is the end of the Law unto righteousness to everyone who believes." He does not say, "Christ is the end of the Law" full stop. Rather, he says that Christ is the end of the law *for righteousness*. That is, he is the only means by which a right standing before God may be attained. However, Paul also says "Do we then overthrow the law by this faith? By no means! On the contrary, we uphold the law." (Romans 3:31). In so doing, far from justifying righteousness rendering the authority of the law null and void, it sustains and confirms it. Our moral obligation to God is strengthened, not weakened, by our relationship to Jesus Christ.

But what role, then, is left for the law in Paul's thinking? Though he is adamant that the law can have no place in establishing an individual's standing before God on the basis of works-righteousness, Paul is clear that the abiding standards of the divine law do define the content of the new obedience that should characterise those in Christ. He sees in the law the expression of the will of God that sets the norms for the new life. "God has done what the law, weakened by the flesh, could not do. By sending his own Son in the likeness of sinful flesh and for sin, he condemned sin in the flesh, *in order that the righteous requirement of the law might be fulfilled in us*, who walk not according to the flesh but according to the Spirit" (Romans 8:3-4).

Walking according to the Spirit solves the problem that the law on its own could not. When he wrote, "The letter kills, but the Spirit gives life" (2 Corinthians 3:6), Paul was not dismissing the law. Even though in the same context he calls it "the ministry of death" (2 Corinthians 3:7) and "the ministry of condemnation" (2 Corinthians 3:9), he still acknowledges that it was glorious because it came from God. However, he views the Mosaic ordinances as essentially external to those who received them, as was typified by their being written on letters of stone. The letter stated God's standards, but could do nothing to incline the heart to obey them. The letter stated God's standards, and can only pronounce condemnation on those who fail to respond to them. (The same is still true of the letter of the gospel. "Among those who are perishing" it proves to be "a fragrance from death to death", 2 Corinthians 2:15-16.) It needs inner Spirit-worked change to empower to faith and so provide access to Christ's remedy for those who have failed to meet the law's demands. This change also impels the believer to a new obedience, not with a view to boasting in one's own achievement, but with a view to expressing gratitude for what one has been given. Viewed from the perspective of the new age and the fulness of the Holy Spirit, the law is no longer an outward written code but, as Jeremiah predicted (Jeremiah 31:33), it is implanted within individuals, written on their hearts. The continuing normativity of the law has not been undermined. It is now transmuted into the new experience of being law-bound to Christ ("not being outside the law of God but under the law of Christ", 1 Corinthians 9:21) and seeking to "fulfil the law of Christ" (Galatians 6:2).

These references that join "law" and "Christ" bring out how clearly Paul realised that it needs a heart filled with love towards Christ and mankind to enter into whole-hearted obedience to that law. Without love the law is external, cold, heartless, a source of condemnation. It does not motivate to obedience. It cannot recover or restore the offender. It can only demand obedience and deliver a verdict of guilty on the offender. But the impulse of love from a heart suffused with gratitude and devotion to Christ for his salvation finds its guidance in the law taught and exemplified by Christ "who gave himself for us to redeem us from all lawlessness and to purify for himself a people for his own possession who are zealous for good works" (Titus 2:14).

And such zeal and love is only engendered by the inworking of the Holy Spirit. There is no disjunction between love and keeping the requirements of the law. There is no antithesis between walking according to the Spirit and observing how God demands we live. Permitting oneself to be led by the Spirit consists in learning afresh to discern and prove the good and acceptable and perfect will of God (Romans 12:2). Christ by his Spirit brings about a new bond to the law in the heart of believers, not as a way of procuring one's own righteousness, but as the road map for a life style that pleases the Saviour whom they love. The indwelling of the Spirit produces the desire to please Christ, the Scripture-based knowledge to imitate him (1 Corinthians 11:1), and the power that enables that desire shaped by knowledge to come to practical expression.

Having seen how Paul views law as functioning in the life of the Christian, it remains for us to consider more closely what the content of that law is. Paul speaks as a minister of a new covenant (2 Corinthians 3:6) whose blessings are extended beyond the confines of Israel because Christ "has broken down in his flesh the dividing wall of hostility by abolishing the law of commandments and ordinances" (Ephesians 2:14-15). He was therefore stoutly opposed to anything that blurred or contradicted the decisive difference between the old age and the new.

But when Paul illustrates specifically how believers ought to conduct themselves it is to the moral law as stated in the Ten Commandments that he turns. "Owe no one anything, except to love each other, for the one who loves another has fulfilled the law. The commandments, 'You shall not commit adultery, You shall not murder, You shall not steal, You shall not covet,' and any other commandment, are summed up in this word: 'You shall love your neighbour as yourself.' Love does no wrong to a neighbour; therefore love is the fulfilling of the law" (Romans 13:8-10). When Paul deals with the ethical problems raised by the Corinthian church, it is to the Old Testament that he goes for orientation and insight (1 Corinthians 5:13; 8:4; 10:11; 14:21). We have already looked at some ways in which this updated application of the abiding principles of the law may be implemented.

However, it is clear that for Paul certain aspects of the Mosaic Law have been superseded. "For neither circumcision counts for anything nor uncircumcision, but keeping the commandments of God"

(1 Corinthians 7:19). The ceremonial aspects of the law (indeed of the Abrahamic covenant) are not of ultimate significance. What really counts and is of first-rate importance is "keeping the commandments of God", and by this Paul is pointing to the moral law as distinct from temporary ceremonial observances. The apostle does not use the category ceremonial law, but in Colossians 2:16-17 he echoes the teachings of Jesus in that he dismisses questions of food and drink, or the observance of a festival or a new moon or a Sabbath as "a shadow of the things to come". Further, when Paul says that Christ our Passover is sacrificed for us (1 Corinthians 5:7), it is obvious that he views the sacrificial system of the Mosaic Law as superseded and effectively ended. But still, there is a clear sense in which law and commandment remain, and that is to be found in the moral law that is the abiding revelation of what God is like in himself and what he requires from everyone everywhere.

The law of liberty

So, then, Jesus and the apostles uphold the law. It has continuing validity until heaven and earth disappear (Matthew 5:18). But it is the law freed from the circumstances and conditions that had relevance only for the Old Testament period and which are no longer appropriate to the age of the new covenant which focuses on the once-for-all sacrifice made by Christ and the right standing before God which he graciously confers on those who trust in him.

There remains another style of objection to the role of the law in the life of the Christian. It is that law is inconsistent with the freedom the believer is to enjoy. Is it not the case that "where the Spirit of the Lord is, there is freedom" (2 Corinthians 3:17), and that "for freedom Christ has set us free" (Galatians 5:1)? Does not James talk of "the perfect law, the law of liberty" (James 1:25)?

Here again we are confronted by a contemporary mode of thought that springs from the basic flaw of fallen human thinking. The sin of mankind is basically one of rebellion against divine authority and of seeking to supplant God's norms with the dictates of human nature. Being free is viewed as a condition where there are no constraints at all on what we may do. Freedom is taken as the lordship of self, rather than the lordship of God. The metaphor of being free as a bird is often employed. We see a bird flying wherever it wants in the sky, going high or low as it pleases, not having to bother with passports or visas to cross international boundaries. Nothing seems to hold it back from doing what it pleases. But that is not so. The flight of the bird cannot defy the laws of gravity. How low it swoops or how high it ascends is dictated by its physical constitution. The life it leads and its survival cannot escape from the demands of the ecological system of which it is part. The wild bird enjoys a liberty that the caged canary does not have, but that liberty is within the parameters set in the created realm. True human liberty is no different.

What James means by "the law of liberty" can best be understood by examining what he says about it a little later in his letter. "If you really fulfil the royal law according to the Scripture, 'You shall love your neighbour as yourself,' you are doing well. But if you show partiality, you are committing sin and are convicted by the law as transgressors. For whoever keeps the whole law but fails in one point has become accountable for all of it. For he who said, 'Do not commit adultery,' also said, 'Do not murder.' If you do not commit adultery but do murder, you have become a transgressor of the law. So speak and so act as those who are to be judged under the law of liberty. For judgment is without mercy to one who has shown no mercy. Mercy triumphs over judgment" (James 2:8-13).

Here again we note that the discussion of law is conducted in terms of the moral law as particularised in the Decalogue. The parameters within which true love displays itself are those that are dictated by the abiding standards of God's moral law. But in this passage James uses an additional term, "the royal law". It is unlikely that the term "royal" refers to the status of the believer as if the injunction was one suited to the life style of those who are truly kings — though that is undoubtedly true. Equally it is improbable that "royal" refers to the status of the law of love as the leading law that is supreme over others, though again that would reflect the message of Scripture. What James is doing is rather to employ the covenant model of the people of God as those who serve a heavenly king. He points to this law as coming from a king, namely Christ. It is the law of the Great King, invested with covenantal authority and given to shape the loyal and grateful response of his people for all that he has done.

The lordship of Jesus Christ is a fundamental truth of Christianity. "Lord" in the name, the Lord Jesus Christ, is no formality, but the recognition of an awesome fact. The response of the heart motivated by love towards him is what the king requires as the expression of love towards him and towards our fellows. "This is my commandment, that you love one another as I have loved you" (John 15:12). This is what constraints the living of his subjects.

But there is also here the reminder that the Lordship of Christ will eventually be displayed in judgment. This king is the judge of the universe. He judges both those who acknowledge his sovereignty and those who do not. As regards those who are his loyal subjects, they will be "judged under the law of liberty". Where there is no law, there is no offence and therefore no ground for judgment. But there is God's moral law and it will be the standard of scrutiny on the day of Christ's return. What then is the law of liberty? Is it a second set of standards that God applies to those who are his people? No, there is one standard, his moral law. That moral law condemns all: none is righteous. But the law of liberty does not vary the standards. It receives them as the royal law of Christ, given not to those who are under law, seeking to work out their own salvation, but given to those called by grace, freed from the oppressive bondage of earning their own salvation and made freedmen in the kingdom of Christ. They are liberated from the thraldom of sin to serve and please him who proclaims liberty to the captives.

True liberty is not licence to do whatever we please. It is the opportunity and empowerment to fulfil the potential with which our Creator has endowed us. It is the recognition that we are no longer canaries in the cage of Satan. Rather, there is now freedom for those loosed by the gospel from the enslavement in which we all naturally find ourselves — freedom to achieve the goals that God has laid down for us and freedom to do so in a way of which he approves. True freedom is not to be found in doing what we determine, but in doing what we ought to do, and in doing what we ought to do willingly and wholeheartedly in conformity to the moral law.

The moral law in today's world

On what basis, then, should the Church urge the relevance of the Ten Commandments in modern society? Our fundamental ground for doing so is not because God gave the Decalogue to Israel at Mount Sinai. The standards of the Decalogue remain relevant for all mankind because they encapsulate the moral law that is from creation. That law is not arbitrary. It is a reflection of God himself. It arises from the character of the deity, and is to be reflected by mankind created as his image and likeness. Mankind has rebelled, but that in no way diminishes the relevance or force of the Maker's instructions.

Now that gives us an angle on how to respond to the individual who says, "You are urging these standards on me, or on society as a whole, but I do not share your Christian commitment. They are not relevant to me. It is wrong-headed and an imposition on your part to expect me to adopt your standards when I do not share your faith commitment." But we are not being inconsistent in our own thinking. While the impulse to obey the moral law and the capacity for doing so has been transformed for the Christian, the standards of the moral law originated before the Fall. Its demands continue to address humanity in general, being based on our answerability to our Creator for our conduct. Here is the true status and dignity of mankind. It is our individual responsibility to account for our behaviour to God who has made known to us the norms by which he will judge.

It is not the case that we should keep silent about our Christian commitment as being the basis of our advocacy of public policies that are in accordance with the standards of God's moral law. Inevitably we must recognise that others will not share our presuppositions, but that does not mean that no progress can be made. The Christian can interact with the non-believer without compromising his commitment to Christ.

It is possible to argue for adherence to the moral law on the basis that its requirements make sense. Because they express the Maker's instructions for mankind. An individual or a society ignores them at their peril. As the Maker's instructions are framed for our good they do not present a distortion of our humanity but a way of realising its highest moral potential. It is possible to construct rational arguments for adherence to these standards in terms of the common good, the well-being of individuals and the welfare of society. That may not be the highest theological ground on which to proceed, but it is not contrary to Scripture. In the realm of common grace, we appeal to the remnants of moral consciousness within mankind. We know that these standards come from God. Given the constitution of human nature and our moral nature, it does not matter what the form of current social or political organisation is, it does not matter what degree of scientific prowess has been displayed or what technological progress has been achieved, our basic nature remains the same. Departure from the Creator's moral standards brings social and ethical confusion, decay and disintegration just as surely as defiance of the physical laws he has impressed on the natural realm leads to disaster. The time scale may not be the same, but the sequence of events may be traced, and moral cause and consequence may be argued as cogently as any scientific discussion. The standards of the Maker's instructions may be confidently urged in the public forum on the grounds of their reasonableness and their explanatory power for understanding social change.

Furthermore, the Christian ought not to be diffident in contending for the standards of the moral law. We should not be hesitant. What we say is derived from Scripture; there is no reason to be unsure. We have every right (as well as the responsibility) to present these standards which are divinely set and which correspond to the way we are constituted. There is also this that we should remember. God has not left himself without the witness of conscience. What is said in accordance with his word and the precepts of the moral law can pierce human defences and bring conviction of its accuracy and relevance.

There are starry-eyed reformers who think that they will transform society by reason of the force of their arguments and the obvious excellence of the goals that their policies seek to implement. But sooner or later — generally sooner — they come up against the hard fact of human fallenness, of the spiritual corruption of the human heart. Those whose policy prescriptions are informed by the standards of the moral law ought to avoid this misconception. Acceptance of the moral law results in constant awareness that mankind has fallen. It is not the case that people will necessarily endorse what is evidently good; there is always the inclination to try to turn any proposal to their own selfish advantage. The Christian policy maker is, however, also in a position to point beyond the letter of policy in the civil realm to the only real and lasting solution to the problem of human fallenness that is provided in the gospel of Jesus Christ. It is possible to work hard to change external conditions — and it is right to do so — but that is dealing with the symptoms of the malaise rather than the fundamental condition, which is that of the human heart.

It is, of course, the case that conforming to the moral law is not salvation. Observance of the law does not save any individual. Those who intervene in public debate on the basis of the moral law are not, as such, presenting the gospel. Furthermore, in this fallen world, we are not to suppose that any success achieved will be permanently maintained. The fallen mind is at enmity with the will of God, and what is gained in one area may be lost in another. Or it may come under renewed assault with the passage of time. But despite all the negatives that may be mentioned, we must never give up in our efforts to testify to God's will for individuals and society. Lessening the offence that human sin and rebellion causes God is truly a Christian service. Lessening the misery and despair caused by individuals and societies to themselves as they act in reckless disregard of God's law is a gospel goal. Both may contribute through divine blessing to even greater good.

Endnotes

[1] Unless otherwise indicated, Scripture quotations are from the English Standard Version (Anglicised edition), Harper Collins Publishers (2002)

[2] The Westminster Confession of Faith, Chapter 19, para. IV

[3] See for instance a discussion of this in Murray, J, *Principles of Conduct*, The Tyndale Press (1957), pages 23-24